T0368424

THE GREATEST
INVESTMENT

RICHARD ZUREKK

WestBow Press books may be ordered through booksellers or by contacting:

WestBow Press
A Division of Thomas Nelson & Zondervan
1663 Liberty Drive
Bloomington, IN 47403
www.westbowpress.com
844-714-3454

ISBN: 979-8-3850-2566-4 (sc)
ISBN: 979-8-3850-2567-1 (e)

Library of Congress Control Number: 2024910078

Print information available on the last page.

WestBow Press rev. date: 07/03/2024

WESTBOW
PRESS®
A DIVISION OF THOMAS NELSON
& ZONDERVAN

FOR EDEN

FOREWORD

Perspectives, we all have them, they are neither good nor bad, only what we do with them can place a qualifier on them. Someone might consider the greatest investment to be Microsoft, Apple, Tesla, Amazon, or Google etc. Another person might consider a water filter for a community to be the greatest, and yet another might consider the time they spent with an important person in their lives to be their greatest investment. God may consider human beings to be the greatest investment. The greatest investment to date is the ability to create clean energy, no matter what your perspective, for the following reasons:

- It is the only type of energy the planet will accept.
- Everyone likes to consume energy.
- It is the next step in energy evolution, perhaps human evolution.
- It will likely mark the end of energy slavery.
- It will perhaps mark the realization that we are the same species and in-fighting is counter-productive at best.

A victory over the fossil fuel industry could mean a triumph for all of humanity and an acceleration of the transition to clean energy. Clean energy production and use is the next step of energy evolution, sadly, the fossil fuel industry clearly feels the benefits of a few shareholders outweighs the needs of the many. It is understandable and disappointing that our governments are not yet meaningfully invested in developing a new way of producing energy. Their delay tactics slowing the migration to clean energy is fundamentally hurting Canada; when the demand for crude oil does start to decline permanently (if it has not already), O.P.E.C members will be the last fossil fuel producers due to their cost of production and quality of product.

The relatively small size of the Canadian economy means that governments have long understood they need to create a crown corporation to accomplish tasks of "vital importance to the Canadian people." Under this tagline Trudeau sold the Trans-Mountain pipeline expansion (TMX) project to the public – Hudson's Bay Company, Canadian National Railway, Air Canada, Bell Canada, Atomic Energy Canada, BC Ferries, and Petro-Canada (to name a few) are or have been Crown Corporations at one time. At this point in time the Government still has two choices: 1. Continue all in on fossil fuels and try to appease the public with green-washing campaigns and meaningless (in an overall sense) green initiatives while subsidizing fossil fuel production 2. Go all in on green energy – particularly green hydrogen. Traditionally it has been a good idea to go all in with the fossil fuel industry, so they bought Trans-Mountain hoping for the best. Interestingly enough, the Federal Government released a report in June 2022 (when the cost was only 21 billion CAD) declaring that the pipeline was worthless, validating what the green movement and I have been saying all along. I have been saying since 2012, that rushing to unload our garbage oil is not good business (ignoring all the other negatives.) In 2018 I wrote a paper showing that we could have built a green hydrogen business, and most of the infrastructure needed, for the cost the cost of one TMX. If created thoughtfully, this would include the creation of demand to justify its existence plus all the associated benefits. Below I detail why TMX has unlimited negatives and green hydrogen has unlimited positives.

If one accepts that good ideas never die, I submit to you that Canada should join the race to create a green hydrogen and clean energy economy and help those already engaged. The writing of this Book is intended to highlight: why it is in our best interest to do so, how this can be accomplished, and why delay magnifies the detrimental effects of continued fossil fuel use (which includes war, highlighting the war in Ukraine). I would like humanity to adopt the most positive global direction; uplifting the majority in long run, not just a few million in the short term.

Three times I have been unemployed for periods greater than 1 week. Just recently I was voluntarily unemployed for 1 day, during which time I was acutely reminded of the stress and negative feelings associated with unemployment (a situation that I would not wish on anyone.) I hope to reach Canadians and show that it is far better to compete as a leader in energy production innovations than trail behind. A few days ago I attended a zoom call that reinforced the argument I present here, during that call some participants involved with the provincial Government mentioned that many representatives were afraid to oppose fossil fuel proliferation because they would be kicked out of the party (in this case the NDP), but also saying specifically that if there were a significant push by the public for green energy, the party would be forced to revisit its energy policies.

For those that like credentials, mine are as follows:

- I attained a Bachelor of Arts from University of Manitoba in History and Economics.
- At the Canadian Securities Institute I held numerous management and financial derivatives certificates
- Working with RBC for 3 years I learned the Canadian personal banking system.
- I also learned the Canadian discount brokerage system, including financial options, working for TD Waterhouse for 3 years.
- I operated as a Commodity Broker with Canadian retail brokers for 8 years, trading all financial products (futures, options, bonds, mutual funds, stocks, GICs) except insurance: during those 8 years I was Assistant Branch Manager for 1.
- I conducted geophysical surveys primarily with Suncor Energy in the oil sands mines in Alberta, Canada.
- I have been employed as an Electrician in the lower mainland since 2019.

TABLE OF CONTENTS

CURRENT MATTERS

All my life I have been in awe of an artist's ability to touch the rest of humanity through their art regardless of origin. I have not spent the time to learn how to create visual or audio art and as a result I am unsurprisingly awful. This is my attempt (in a medium I am relatively competent in) to share with humanity a skill I am very good at, following trends to forecast the future. I estimate that I have been correct roughly 80% of the time when predicting long term events.

The keys to ending climate change are out there but sadly and unsurprisingly many jurisdictions are still heavily influenced by the oil industry. Not only will I show you why but allow me to show you how green hydrogen and clean energy can become our primary energy sources. I will use Canada's current economic and political climate as an example.

We are currently bearing witness to the inevitable decline of the oil industry juggernaut and its herculean effort to stifle the transition to clean, sustainable energy production by mustering all their political influence to delay transition efforts they are decelerating energy evolution and exacerbating climate change. Hopefully this book will play some part (however slight) in speeding up the adoption of clean energy. I dare hope to live long enough to see the smiling faces enjoying a life free of environmental anxiety.

Sadly, the oil industry is resisting meaningful change even though the prevailing trend is toward clean energy and their efforts are creating counter winds (1). The oil lobbyists have been so effective recently that the Organization of Petroleum Exporting Companies (O.P.E.C.) revised its oil demand projection to actually increase 16% by 2045. Given the projection is driven by data (action not words) this updated scenario is likely; but the winds of change can easily blow in the other direction changing the outlook accordingly. The longer we allow the oil industry to encumber the transition to alternative sources the more damage is being done to the environment compounding unnecessary suffering for future generations (2).

While the transition to clean energy is inevitable, how fast that will occur remains to be seen. It is this unknown timeframe that begs the questions:

- How much more damage will occur?
- How many people will unnecessarily perish?
- How much more of our home will be needlessly destroyed?

How much more of our precious, limited resources will be utterly squandered on unnecessary in-fighting and foolish infrastructure projects by accepting green-washing, propaganda, and inaction. I write with the hopes that my explanation is enticing enough to encourage you to say: "Yes! I would welcome climate stability, prosperity for humanity, and a brighter future for us all!"

THE BASICS

By my definition, climate stability is basically a return to the climate we experienced before the turn of the century.

Climate events that were rare prior to 2018 have now become commonplace, exemplified in the language we now use in climate conversations terms such as:

- Atmospheric rivers (AR (3)),
- Extreme drought
- Abnormal heat (4)

Most of the human population believe that nobody should have to live in fear by suffering from food insecurity, a lack of proper housing or struggle to access clean air and water. Multi-pronged discrimination need not exist yet we still struggle to address any of these issues. What is diverting our attention? There is no good reason for future generations to suffer from further unnecessary delays. I suggest that the move to clean energy will go a long way to solving some of those issues and it should be done before the climate and the price of crude oil collapse. Is it time for the next revolution?

What you need to know about how we use energy

Electricity production for the grid that serves most of the planet can be classified in two categories:

1. Baseline or Base load energy is on all the time and typically slow to change.
   Examples are:
   - Coal plants
   - Nuclear plants
   - Hydro plants
   - Methane (Natural Gas) plants
   - Combined cycle plant - a fossil gas fired plant that also uses some of the heat from the exhaust gases.
   - Geothermal
   - Biomass / Biogas

2. Fluctuating Energy Production
    *   Wind
    *   Solar
    *   Wave

Fossil-burning baseline power plants are the workhorses of energy production and produce up to an estimated 40% of CO_2 emissions (2022). They are the low hanging fruit which can enable us to meet and exceed carbon reduction targets because they do not move and necessary immobile infrastructure can be assembled nearby. The other 60% of emissions are attributed to non-baseline applications which can be further subdivided in multiple ways.

Green hydrogen can supply all energy needs however, it may be more efficient to use another form of clean energy; for example, because of the weight to output ratio, it is currently more efficient to use battery technology to power passenger cars and more efficient to use hydrogen fuel cells in large vehicles such as semi-trucks, buses, mining equipment.

Like gasoline, methane (NG), coal, kerosene, and propane etc., hydrogen is just a way of storing energy, the difference being that hydrogen is found almost everywhere in the universe and it can be produced and used without the negative repercussions seen in all fossil fuel production. Hydrogen can be used at any time, in any location, and can be adapted for all energy applications. I believe we are only stepping into the start of an enormous learning curve – think the sun.

Using fossil fuels to explore beyond the moon's orbit is blatantly impractical. We also now know that using fossil fuels has multiple negative ramifications, that they are finite, and their utility is crawling to an end.

> "The fact that if done correctly, the transition will benefit EVERYONE and none need lose a penny or wink of sleep." Did it occur to anyone?

> "as each has received a gift," we are to "use it to serve one another, as good stewards of God's varied grace" (1 Peter 4:10).

Oh right… the me, me, me culture and the worship of false Gods, in this case money.

You make a difference!

Looking toward the school field across from my apartment, I catch the neighborhood kids creating a snowperson and pause to reminisce over my public exchanges over the last few weeks. Whether I was taking my daughter skating amongst the mostly under thirteen crowd at the public rink, jogging around the neighborhood, or working at the nearby university, the common thread holding them in my heart is hope.

Science has been telling us for years that we need to change the way we do things. If it is denial, ignorance, or our narcissistic belief in our infallibility; the need to remain positive -especially when faced with circumstances beyond our control- is paramount. In my mind, it is better to try to positively affect those circumstances with the influence you have. You can choose:

- What you drive
- What you eat
- Who you vote for

Only you can control what you do.

Yes, things are tough, and many people are having trouble making ends meet; you can't afford an EV (electric vehicle), organic food, or hemp clothes. Understandable. You may feel your personal contribution to carbon emissions are minute compared to the whole. Every little change matters!

YOU CAN VOTE FOR THE GREEN PARTY OF CANADA

Why, you ask?

A significant shift in support away from business as usual will send a message to politicians that their job is on the line, specifically regarding their opinion on energy use and production. This can be applied in most jurisdictions including the U.S. due to the candidacy of Cornel West and the growing presence of the U.S. Green Party.

THE PLATFORMS

The optics of a clear alternative to the status quo are not always available and, in that event, not voting does become an option. At this time Canadians are fortunate to have a clear voting alternative to the status quo as noted below.

The Conservative Party of Canada represents rich Canadians. While there is no platform currently on their website to reference here is Poilievre's acceptance speech (5) which includes: tax cuts, cutting social spending, and more tax cuts as well as a thinly veiled threat to indigenous people "It's my way or the highway."

The Liberal Party of Canada represents primarily rich Canadians who have a conscience. They try to appeal to the rest of Canadians by buying their vote and making enticing promises (knowing some of them are outright lies (6),) such as their current climate policies which are largely meaningless if they continue to support fossil fuel production -particularly the expansion of LNG (liquid natural gas) and oil-sands production.

The New Democratic Party of Canada primarily represent the working class in Canada and have repeatedly tried to position themselves as friends or representatives of the "Green" movement in Canada. Since the backlash to the Notley Government and its evident failure, it seems that they have hopped directly into bed with the fossil fuel industry and remained loyal to their core followers (7). They say they remain committed to fostering a clean environment but have supported the Liberal government's decision to build the TMX and Coastal Gas Link (CGL) pipelines. Their actions do not support their words.

The Green Party of Canada have their values listed on the website: https://www.greenparty.ca/en/green-values

Voting for the Green Party will let fellow humans know that you care about the environment regardless of your economic stature and send a message to the political juggernauts to "meaningfully" address the problem or suffer further decline.

If we continue to choose the status quo, why should we expect any progress? Let's start down the road to helping the next generation create sustainable and environmentally harmonious choices rather than letting the same old lobbyists and ineffectual Government "represent" the people, not the corporations.

While there is no guarantee that electing the Green Party will address any of the problems we currently face, what IS guaranteed is that electing any other parties will allow continued inaction, inevitably defaulting to what is easiest - hopping into bed with the fossil fuel industry.

Don't believe me!

Pete Townsend and The Who are far more eloquent.

"Meet the new boss.

Same as the old boss"

-The Who, *Won't get fooled again*

THE PREVAILING FEAR

In all fairness, there is a great deal of fear when departing from the tried-and-true formula of "get into bed with the fossil fuel industry and all will be well." Now the planet's rapidly changing environment is forcing us to live cleaner, smarter and do better. I have no doubt that we will eventually change and adapt to the situation; necessity is the mother of invention. I am advocating for a faster change to minimize the negative effects and maximize the positive by trying to highlight the fact that most people don't need to do anything except DEMAND that change.

As this technology is already being developed in foreign countries, we cannot delay our transition. If we continue to put off the migration to clean energy there is greater risk that workers in the oil industry will not be able to secure a job within the clean energy sector. The longer this transition is delayed the larger the gap will widen as foreign workers become more highly skilled and educated endangering more and more Canadian jobs -especially those farther up the ladder.

I have accepted the idea that all Canadian economics schools are not incompetent. They are either afraid of speaking out against the oil industry or feel that the negative blowback (which can be significant in Canada now) is enough to stifle the most obvious: "it is not a good idea to build one of the world's most expensive pieces of infrastructure (TMX) in an environment where failure is guaranteed." The real tragedy is that the Canadian oil sands companies will be the first to go bankrupt (not-withstanding subsidies) and the numerous negative aspects will continue:

- Indirectly knowingly killing people (8)
- Directly killing the land (9)
- Blatantly ignoring people and landowners (10)
- Ignoring a Government report declaring TMX worthless (11)

The overall damage to our environment is incalculable.

The planet's thermal moderators (glaciers) will disappear soon, and it is likely the full effects of climate change will be felt. Where I am it gets uncomfortably hot in the summer and the variations are constantly increasing, for example, we are now suffering from wildfires in the middle of winter and extreme weather later in the various seasons.

In case you haven't noticed, I'd like to share a short story with you as an example.

When I was growing up on the northern edge of the Canadian prairie through the 70's, 80's, 90's and even 2000's you could set your calendar by the weather. The first snow came on Halloween, give or take a day or two, and and the weather was -20C° to -40C° until April with very little variation. I really started to notice after 2008 (perhaps earlier) when Winnipeg started to experience one full week of -50C° in January or February every year. Now it is common that temperatures on the prairie fluctuate during the winter between +5C° and -50C° -this year it was around 0C° in central Manitoba in November! I could go on but I'm sure you get the point.

Is it ironic or fitting that current Government and economic structures are failing to address our most acute challenges highlighting their inherent weaknesses and the need to improve them?

In the immortal words of Geddy Lee and Rush:

> "He's noble enough to know what's right
> But weak enough not to choose it
> He's wise enough to win the world
> But fool enough to lose it —
> He's a New World man…"
> -Rush, *New World Man*

Here are a few time lapse photos of glaciers around the world.

Agassiz Glacier

1913
WC Alden, USGS Photographic Library

2007
D Fagre, USGS

Credit: USGS U.S. Geological Survey

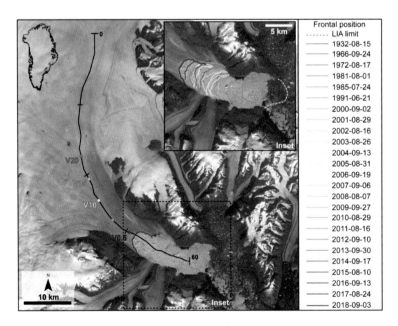

Citation: Brough S, Carr JR, Ross N and Lea JM (2019) Exceptional Retreat of Kangerlussuaq Glacier, East Greenland, Between 2016 and 2018. *Front. Earth Sci.* 7:123. doi: 10.3389/feart.2019.00123

Credit: USGS U.S. Geological Survey

Logan & Red Eagle Glaciers

1914
EC Stebinger, USGS Photo Library

2009
L McKeon, USGS

Credit: USGS U.S. Geological Survey

Boulder Glacier

1910
M Elrod, GNP Archives

2007
D Fagre / G Pederson, USGS

Credit: USGS U.S. Geological Survey

Photo 10: Mount Edith Cavell, Alberta, Canada 1984

Credit: Dave Price

If you look up recent photos you will see significant retreat.

ANXIETY

It has brought me to a place of realization that everything made by man will disappear and everything made by God will endure long after we are gone.

I pin the roots of my anxiety on the 3 perceptions that shaped my worldview up until 2010 or so.

Perception 1:

There is a difference between the Canadian political parties and, generally, Canadian politics is less corrupt than other jurisdictions. As a young, impressionable, type A personality (12), I believed the propaganda put forward by the Canadian centre-right and became active in the Conservative Party of Canada. To make a long story short, I spent 6 years intentionally preparing to run as a Federal Member of Parliament (MP) in the riding of Winnipeg Centre and did in 2006. Twice during the campaign, the president of the Conservative party came to see me, each time he asked me not to try to win. At the time, I was confused by this and felt that I was not going to discard 6 years of preparation. When they realized that I was not going to stop trying, they fired me and got another candidate. Upon reflection, they already knew that they were going to win the election and were likely trying to see if I would do what I was told, even if I disagreed. Perception 1, I left in a dumpster on Kenaston boulevard.

Perception 2:

The public trading markets are largely fair to all participants. (FYI, I was employed in the financial industry from 1998 to 2011.) On this particular subject I could go on for hours, some of which is documented in my book: *319%*. Stock markets, for example, heavily favour the rich (as does much of our current economic system.) Typically, the higher up the career ladder you go, the worse the corruption gets (13). Anyway, the final straw for me came in 2008 when Wall Street stole 16 trillion USD from the U.S. taxpayer (my business partner and I knew exactly what they were doing and predicted the ending with precision.) Perception 2 and my career in finance were thrown promptly in the garbage.

Perception 3:

People will choose what is best for humanity, country, or corporation if that choice doesn't affect their standard of living. Growing up I felt the Lord always gave me what I needed (sometimes more, but never less) and so I perceived the majority of people operated along the lines of altruistic research (14).

This perception was gradually eroded starting with the 2008 financial crisis and has been continually disappointing me since. I still hope, believe, and pray that our true nature is altruistic; current affairs being the summation of an education system and our culture largely being based on capitalism (a predatory system designed to favour the rich) has made it very difficult to maintain this perception.

Living in one of Canada's most populous cities, I have observed the transformation of a small city to a big city, the connection? I find this outlook brave but at the same time I realize that living life with a positive outlook is healthy and desirable. Having lived with severe anxiety for 7 years (2012-2019), I am acutely aware of living without hope and the effect it has on those around you.

Luke 16:11
"If then you have not been faithful in the unrighteous wealth,
who will entrust to you the true riches?"

PROPAGANDA

"End of passion play, crumbling away
I'm your source of self-destruction
Veins that pump with fear, sucking darkest clear
Leading on your death's construction
Taste me you will see
More is all you need
You're dedicated to
How I'm killing you
Come crawling faster
Obey your master
Your life burns faster
Obey your master
Master"
-Metallica, *Master of Puppets*

Metallica is not my favourite band, but they have produced some masterpieces and *Master of Puppets* is truly a work of art. Even if you do not like metal music, I encourage you to read the entire lyrics online.

It remains difficult for people to distinguish between a truly positive direction or a bad idea because of widespread propaganda. The current system encourages and rewards behaviors geared to the individual at the expense of others, sometimes even to the individual. Looking at the roots of modern propaganda is useful in understanding how we have come to a place where it is so difficult to distinguish good information from bad. Luckily Naomi Oreskes and Erik Conway precisely explain this in their novels *The Merchants of Doubt* and *The Big Myth*, but I will provide you with a summary and encourage you to read the books to really grasp the size of the problem.

Perhaps ironically, it seems that at the beginning of the 20th century the National Electric Light Association (NELA) really developed the playbook of disinformation closely followed by the tobacco, chemical, and now, fossil fuel industries.

Their efforts included, but were not limited to:

- Creating and directing institutes to conduct "research" that puts their activities in a good light.
- Buying or offering to buy textbooks for school institutions.
- Trumpeting their "research" in popular magazines.

- Paying seemingly credible sources to create "research."
- Buying highly visible ad space, knowing the product they are selling is harmful to individuals.
- Using said "research" to create an environment of inaction.
  and
- Paying politicians to do their bidding.

It truly is insidious how such blatant disregard for others is a recurring theme throughout history; I am looking forward to the time when we all start to work together.

Until then, here are three Canadian activities that exemplify the use of this propaganda:

1. Carbon capture technology is being represented by the oil companies as a viable option to solving climate change. They have such faith in the technology that they are not willing to pay for it themselves. This technology exists and it may have a role to play in the solution, however, it is just a bad idea from several perspectives. At best, it is a low probability solution which gives the people unwilling to change a weak scientific argument to justify their preference not to change, it creates enough doubt in many minds to halt any action that is required.

2. The TMX is a subsidy that has **no** positive aspects and yet the Canadian public continues to fund the detrimental project; the chief selling point being it would create many jobs and bring many financial benefits to Canada. They claim there will be profits, but a 2020 study (15) done by the Federal Government itself valued TMX at zero (16)when it cost 21 billion CAD. As of Mar 3, 2024, it is still incomplete with costs now exceeding 34 billion CAD. The total cost will probably approach 40 billion CAD; will it be twice as worthless upon completion? Most of the work is done so many of those are jobs are gone and oil sands producers continue to lay off more workers (17). Finally, while it is likely that the price of crude oil will exceed 50.00 USD / bbl. in the short term, it is also likely in the medium term to fall below 50.00 USD and it is INEVITABLE in the long run, meaning Canadian Oil Sands producers will be losing money.

3. https://www.nationalobserver.com/2024/03/05/news/calls-mount-crackdown-false-fossil-fuel-ads The Provincial Government of British Columbia is intentionally misleading the public by conducting an ad campaign claiming "that LNG is somehow a green source of energy aligned with net zero targets." National Observer

LIQUID NATURAL GAS (LNG)

Natural gas is 70% - 90% methane and raw methane is a powerful greenhouse gas; its use is arguably more detrimental than coal. Per unit of energy, when burned, natural gas produces around 50% of the CO_2 emitted by coal. Before methane is burned, its production suffers from both accidental and intentional leaks. As shown in Table ES-1 below, raw natural gas is 28 times as effective as CO_2 so any gains in the amount of carbon emissions are likely offset by leakage. Assuming the industry has always intentionally underreported emissions of all sorts, any gains in the fight against climate change are entirely fictional. Switching to natural gas does not get us ahead in the fight against climate change, at best there might be a slight improvement, but there is a high probability it is doing more damage than coal.

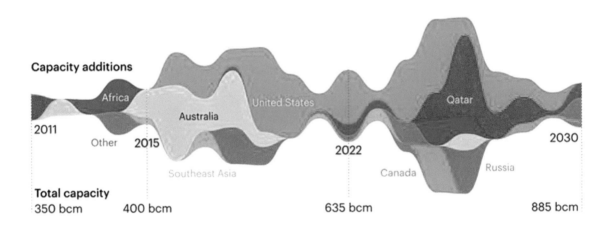

Chart 1: International Energy Agency; World Energy Outlook

What can we do about it in Canada? We can increase surveillance and tax profits from natural gas exploitation based on a leakage rate which is monitored by an independent monitoring agency and a different auditor chosen by the U.N. For example, any leakage rate that negates the positive effect of CO_2 reduction would incur a tax penalty of 50% or more. Given the massive increase in supply coming online now (indicated by Figure 1) the price will likely remain low and demand fairly static; in contrast, the demand for clean energy will significantly increase and supply will struggle to keep up.

OPPORTUNITY AWAITS

——◄○►——

"Star Trek was an attempt to say that humanity will reach maturity and wisdom on the day that it begins not just to tolerate but take a special delight in differences in ideas and differences in life forms."

- Gene Roddenberry

"You have to find something that you love enough to jump over hurdles and break through the brick walls."

- George Lucas

Two of the most successful stories ever recounted to humanity stimulate our thirst for the exploration of our surroundings and directly and indirectly motivate much of our activity. The success of these stories highlights our shared innate curiosity. If we want to regularly reach beyond Earth's atmosphere, we must adopt a more powerful and efficient source of energy. To give credit where credit is due, fossil fuels are largely responsible for providing us with energy and have powered many advances up to this point in time; however, it is also very evident that their continued use is detrimental to our civilization and almost entirely unnecessary.

The list of reasons why fossil fuels are no longer a viable fuel source is long; foremost is the degradation to our one and ONLY environment, alternatives exist -and are becoming increasingly available- that do not degrade our environment. The utility of fossil fuels is maximized or close to it. The probability of finding more fossil fuel beyond this planet's atmosphere is close to zero. On the other hand, hydrogen is the most abundant element in the universe making it a viable option for use in interstellar travel.

The movement to clean energy makes me spine-tinglingly excited to try and live symbiotically with our environment and ensure we have a home for our species to flourish. Imagine a world nicely balanced, humanity living harmoniously with one another and our environment. Looking at the state of the world today one might call me out of touch to dream of such a scenario; I would argue that it is inevitable, and the only question is whether it will take 50 or 500 years to get there. Good ideas never die, they may be delayed or seemingly unrealized, but at some point, the idea of a stable, safe human home will re-surface.

Green hydrogen is the technological solution to many of our current problems. I would go further saying that it is the solution to all our energy related problems, bearing in mind that other forms of energy generation may also fill a complementary role. It is only a matter of time before hydrogen technology can pass the "Grandma test" (when Grandma can go to the local store and pick up a bottle of hydrogen like we do propane) -granted this may be quite a way away- then again maybe not.

Hydrogen is clearly God's favourite form of energy, don't believe me? Look Up! (Or as the case may be, Don't Look Up ;).

There is no longer any reason that we should shit in our own backyard to sustain ourselves and progress. Technology exists now to accomplish any energy related task without the negative impacts of using fossil fuels. If we are serious about solving climate change and taking the next step in human evolution, all renewables in particular green hydrogen will play a central role.

According to the European Geosciences Union

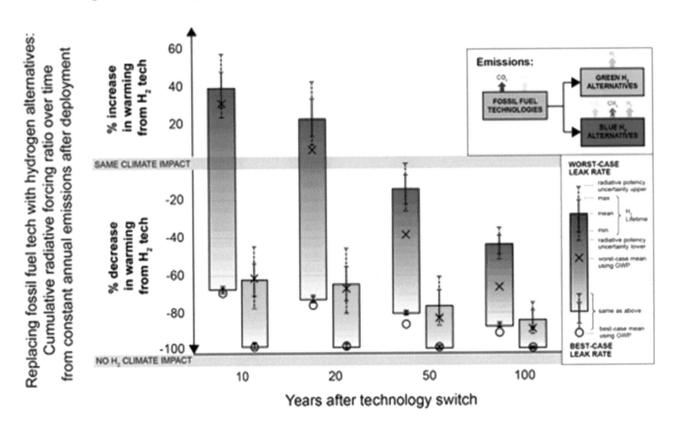

Chart 2: Emission changes over years after switching to hydrogen energy, European Geosciences

Only green hydrogen will improve our situation over time while conveying all the benefits of fossil fuels ... guaranteed... Even if we sustain maximum estimated leakage, we can still be solving climate change using today's technology and simultaneously switch to green hydrogen production.

If the opportunity is a guaranteed winner, then what is the hold up?

In Canada, it is likely that the Canadian majority does not recognize the opportunity. The more time passes, the less Canadians will profit from the "new" energy industry. Clearly Europe, the Biden administration, China, India, S. Korea, Australia and Japan and others acknowledge its UNLIMITED potential. As this technology matures, I am sure they will willingly charge us for their expertise when the time comes for us to adopt a better way.

The Canadian oil industry is detrimentally harming Canada by delaying our entry into this race:

1. Using propaganda to create enough doubt, creating inaction.
2. Denying Canadians high paying long-term jobs within Canada.
3. Squandering resources on worthless, self-serving ventures (What will it be for TMX? $40B?
4. Squandering more resources on self-serving ventures which will amplify the damage done by climate change – all LNG related projects.
5. Squandering even more resources to low probability projects that give the appearance they are addressing the problem – all carbon capture projects.

How do we make the change?

Using the current economic and political system in Canada, I will show how we cannot just profit but prosper by switching to clean energy, particularly green hydrogen.

Let us first grab the low hanging fruit, specifically:

- Converting the last remaining fossil fuel power plants to green energy power plants.
- Converting fossil fuel subsidies to clean energy subsidies.
- Raising taxes on all new equipment that uses fossil fuel.
- Upgrading all governments' fossil fuel burning vehicles to vehicles that only use clean energy.
- Blending hydrogen with natural gas to use in current infrastructure.
- Encouraging heavy industry to use hydrogen powered equipment.

Concurrently, we can start the more long-term projects like:

- building green hydrogen production plants, pipelines and related infrastructure converting existing plants where possible and building new plants in strategically sound sites.
- building a spaceport in Northern Alberta on the land destroyed by oil-sands mining.
- overbuilding the plants in areas where it can be easily exported such as: the Vancouver lower mainland, the St. Lawrence seaway, and Northern Manitoba.

When domestic demand has been sated, export the rest. The customers are already lined up!

- US
- China
- Europe
- Japan
- India

Further demand can be created by offering jurisdictions an option where Canadians can build hydrogen power plants in exchange for long term supply contracts.

The demand is GUARANTEED and like other renewables, the costs associated with green hydrogen use will fall and the effects of climate change will be mitigated!

The three locations mentioned above all have an abundance of the ingredients necessary for significant green hydrogen production and export: fresh water, renewable energy (installed or available), and easy access for export. Steps to convert the Coastal Gaslink pipeline and TMX should be undertaken immediately, then perhaps the effort and resources put into those projects won't be wasted.

It is also important to note that while it may be tempting to immediately raise taxes on gasoline, I don't believe that is the best strategy. A fuel tax increase should be telegraphed to the public, for example an extra 5% tax on gasoline should be implemented in 2 years and every year thereafter. Interestingly Canada's Carbon tax was applied across all of Canada in early 2024 and has been met with significant opposition since 2018 when the Greenhouse Gas Pollution Pricing Act (GGPPA) was passed. Is six years enough lead time? I believe so considering the gravity of the climate crisis and our human tendency to prefer the status quo. Action is required and if that is what it takes to pull your head out of the oil-sands … so be it.

Implement an immediate increase in insurance for gasoline\diesel burning chattels that would look like this,

A 4-cylinder vehicle = no change to current costs
A 6-cylinder vehicle = 1.5 times current costs
An 8-cylinder vehicle = 2 times current costs
A 12-cylinder vehicle = 3 times current costs

As you can see this should not affect low-income owners by giving them time to convert and would encourage high-income people to switch. The money collected from the rich could be given to the poor to make EV ownership easier and support clean energy. Yes I am serious about addressing climate change and having users continue to pay by partially subsidizing the bill for the damage they have caused and partially helping with the transition. I hope people eventually adopt the perspective "I can afford to support efforts that will improve others lives and am proud to do it!" Having said that, if you had any thoughts other than, "I have to vote for the Green party!" please review the chapter "You make a Difference!"

THE DANGER

A book primarily on green hydrogen would be negligent to not include the full picture from all perspectives so here are the dangers associated with using hydrogen.

Raw hydrogen is a greenhouse gas and that is why most models include differing levels of leakage in the hydrogen life cycle. In a very recent study, past research of its kind confirms that the global warming potential (GWP) of hydrogen is 11.4 (+/-2.8%.)

Using the U.S. as an example, the following tables and charts give you an overall picture of how hydrogen compares to other greenhouse gases.

Table ES-1: Global Warming Potentials (100-Year Time Horizon) Used in this Report

Gas	GWP
CO_2	1
CH_4[a]	28
N_2O	265
HFCs	up to 12,400
PFCs	up to 11,100
SF_6	23,500
NF_3	16,100
Other Fluorinated Gases	See Annex 6

[a] The GWP of CH_4 includes the direct effects and those indirect effects due to the production of tropospheric ozone and stratospheric water vapor. The indirect effect due to production of CO_2 is not included. See Annex 6 for additional information.
Source: IPCC (2013).

Table 1: Table ES-1: Global Warming Potentials, U.S. Environmental Protection Agency

If you are wondering where we use the above gasses here is list of common application for each one.

"Agricultural soil management, wastewater treatment, stationary sources of fuel combustion, and manure management are the major sources of N2O emissions. Emissions of substitutes for ozone depleting substances are the primary contributor to aggregate hydrofluorocarbon (HFC) emissions. Perfluorocarbon (PFC) emissions are primarily attributable to electronics manufacturing, fluorochemical production, and primary aluminum production. Electrical equipment systems account for most sulfur hexafluoride (SF6) emissions. The electronics industry is the only source of nitrogen trifluoride (NF3) emissions."

Matteo B. Bertagni, Stephen W. Pacala, Fabien Paulot & Amilcare Porporato wrote "Risk of the hydrogen economy for atmospheric methane" in the journal Nature Giving us a quantifiable explanation why green hydrogen is far superior to blue hydrogen. They state, "For hydrogen referred to as green hydrogen, which is produced by splitting water into hydrogen and oxygen using electricity from renewable sources, Bertagni said that the critical threshold for hydrogen emissions sits at around 9%. That means that if more than 9% of the green hydrogen produced leaks into the atmosphere—whether that be at the point of production, sometime during transport, or anywhere else along the value chain—atmospheric methane would increase over the next few decades, canceling out some of the climate benefits of switching away from fossil fuels.

And for blue hydrogen, which refers to hydrogen produced via methane reforming with subsequent carbon capture and storage, the threshold for emissions is even lower. Because methane itself is the primary input for the process of methane reforming, blue hydrogen producers must consider direct methane leakage in addition to hydrogen leakage. For example, the researchers found that even with a methane leakage rate as low as 0.5%, hydrogen leakages would have to be kept under around 4.5% to avoid increasing atmospheric methane concentrations."

Matteo B. Bertagni, Stephen W. Pacala, Fabien Paulot & Amilcare Porporato (18)

Coupled with leakage monitoring, clearly green hydrogen production is most desirable.

The importance of availability of green hydrogen

"The worry is the Americans. If we meet the right sort, this will work. We get some Buckaroo..."
- Captain Ramius (Sean Connery) in The Hunt for Red October

Even though Sean Connery was British, this quote describes our current situation perfectly.

Within the next 2 years demand for crude oil will peak and then begin to decline permanently. At some point on this curve, it will become more profitable for O.P.E.C. to be the sole supplier of crude oil and they will increase production driving down prices until most of the competition is gone. First up to go bankrupt.... you guessed it, high- cost producers. The timing of such a move will be interesting because the U.S. support provided to Saudi Arabia may delay such a move. It is more likely that O.P.E.C. will no longer agree to more production cuts in an effort to support crude oil prices at which point the prices will fall with demand and gradually all non-O.P.E.C. producers will shift their focus or go bankrupt.

Let there be no question in your mind as to who will be producing crude oil for those applications we cannot substitute: O.P.E.C. has the best quality oil and the lowest production cost in the world.

This leaves a lot of non-O.P.E.C. workers looking for work as well as declining resources to deal with the larger expenditures required by the increasing intensity of climate change. The U.S., currently being the largest exporter of crude oil, is poised to suffer the most from this event and should Donald J. Trump (buckaroo) become president again, it is very likely he will choose to face this event by initiating more violence in a manner that increases the price of crude oil. Hopefully we end up with anyone else but regardless of who becomes president, an increase in the availability of green hydrogen will assist the growth of the U.S hydrogen economy creating jobs while decreasing carbon emissions.

Assisting the Europeans in achieving energy security should help decrease the popularity of radicals and reaffirm our commitment as useful allies. Most notably in India and China, the availability of green hydrogen will have a direct effect on the amount of greenhouse gases they emit. Both countries have already made significant investments in clean energy production but also still rely on fossil fuel energy to meet demand. While both countries appear to be open to green energy, they still rely heavily on Russia to supply their fossil fuel energy. If Canadians were to be net suppliers of green energy to the rest of the world others might think twice before resorting to violence knowing that we will likely stop supplying them with energy. As I mentioned earlier, it is very likely that the Keystone XL pipeline project would be resurrected if it were designed to carry green hydrogen.

Energy security is the central topic of this time and green hydrogen can deliver. Canada just happens to have the resources necessary to help others achieve their goals:

- Energy security
- Food security
- Reduction or elimination of the negative aspects of fossil fuel use
- Addressing Climate Change
- Saving the environment

With 5 years it is very likely that exporting oil from the Canadian oil sands will become unprofitable: in the long run unprofitability is guaranteed. A great majority of the infrastructure that will be needed will take roughly 5 years to build. We will likely build it anyway when the majority realize the opportunity, the only difference being that foreigners will mostly benefit:

- High-paying jobs, they will have the experience, knowledge, and expertise.
- profits
- decide whom is to benefit (who to sell to or not, how to use the profits)

Why not start now? Establish a Crown Corporation!

THE CUSTOMERS

———◆○◆———

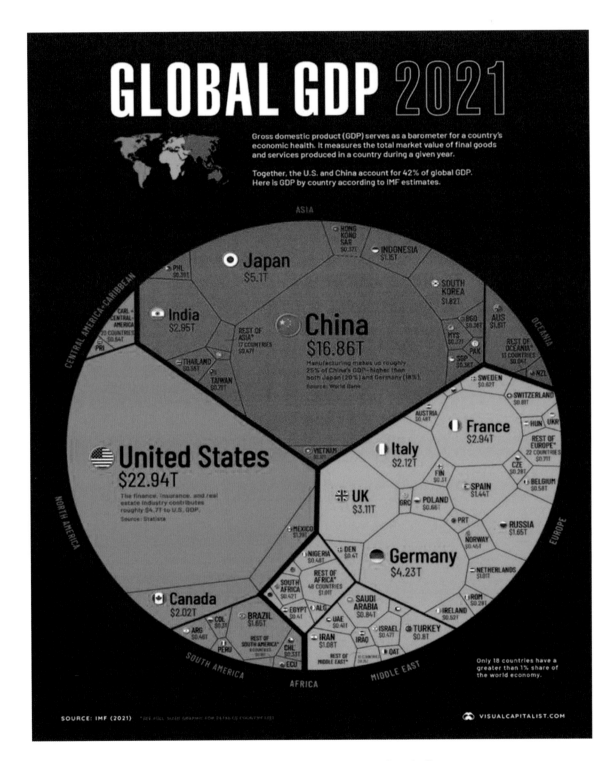

Chart 3: Global GDP 2021, Visual Capitalist

24

Everyone is a potential customer as we all like to consume energy! Some have the capacity to quickly change how they produce and use energy. For those not so blessed we can build clean energy power plants in exchange for long term supply contracts. The amount of wealth generated through selling green hydrogen will make philanthropy necessary, easy, and fulfilling.

Table 5.1 ▷ **Key economic and energy indicators by region/country, 2022**

	Population (million)	Total energy supply (EJ)	Electricity demand (kWh per capita)	Cars per thousand people	CO$_2$ emissions (Gt)	CO$_2$ emissions (t per capita)
United States	336	94	12 133	682	4.7	14
Latin America and the Caribbean	658	37	2 253	137	1.7	3
European Union	449	56	5 521	557	2.7	6
Africa	1 425	36	508	25	1.4	1
Middle East	265	36	4 190	175	2.1	8
Eurasia	238	42	5 051	193	2.4	10
China	1 420	160	5 612	201	12.1	9
India	1 417	42	926	31	2.6	2
Japan and Korea	177	29	8 703	490	1.7	9
Southeast Asia	679	30	1 592	63	1.7	3

Note: EJ = exajoules; kWh = kilowatt-hours; Gt = gigatonnes; t = tonnes.

Table 2: Key economic and energy indicators by region/country, 2022, International Energy Agency

US

The U.S. is traditionally within the top 10 consumers of energy on the planet; you can see their appetite for fossil fuels maxed out in 2013 at around 70% of the electricity generated that year; in 2021 fossil fuels accounted for 60% of the power generated in the US.

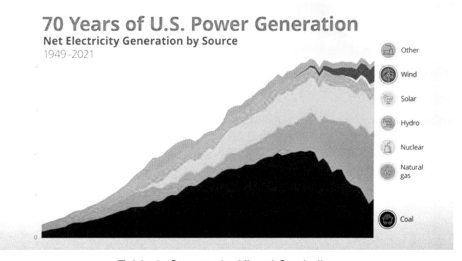

Table 3: Source the Visual Capitalist

https://decarbonization.visualcapitalist.com/animated-70-years-of-u-s-electricity-generation-by-source/

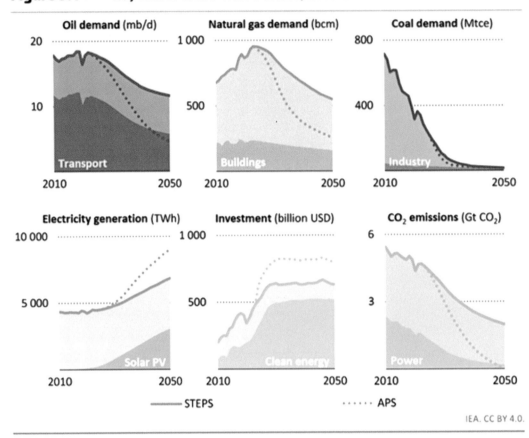

Figure 5.1 ▷ **Key trends in the United States, 2010-2050**

Chart 4: Key trends in the United States, 2010 – 2050, International Energy Agency

Most projections put U.S. energy demand increasing slightly with the difference being made up by renewable production sources and the use of fossil fuel energy remaining constant. That does not mean that the declining demand for fossil fuels cannot be hastened. The Americans are just as interested as the Europeans in energy security and given their proximity supplying excess green energy would be cheaper and easier. Their interest in green energy (under President Biden anyway) is keen, they are developing new technologies so quickly that I am having difficulty staying on top of all the innovation. Assuming the "buckaroo" is not re-elected, it is likely they will reach their stated goal of producing green hydrogen at the cost $US 1/ kg sooner than competitors.

It bears repeating that at some point the U.S. demand curve for oil will plummet because cleaner ways of meeting those energy needs are desirable, a couple of significant recent events pointing in that direction are:

1. Biden indefinitely paused the approval of new LNG projects
2. Cancelation of the proposed Keystone XL pipeline

If the Keystone XL project were designed to carry green hydrogen it would be built in haste. It is very likely that further pipeline projects to carry green hydrogen would follow but that would be dependent on Canadian capacity.

China

Figure 1: China's population in perspective, Visual Capitalist

5.8 China

5.8.1 Key energy and emissions trends

Figure 5.19 ▷ **Key trends in China, 2010-2050**

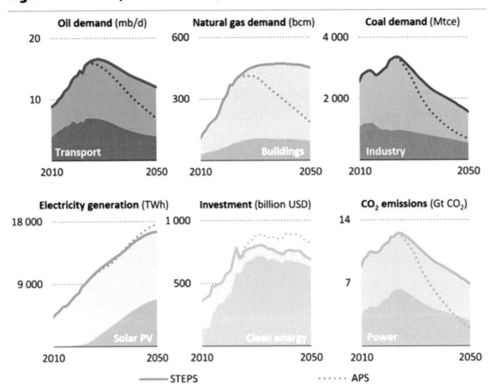

Chart 5: Key trends in China, 2010 – 2050, International Energy Agency

"Momentum behind China's economic growth is ebbing and there is greater downside potential for fossil fuel demand if it slows further. In our scenarios, China's GDP growth averages just under 4% per year to 2030. This results in its total energy demand peaking around the middle of this decade, with robust expansion of clean energy putting overall fossil fuel demand and emissions into decline. If China's near-term growth were to slow by another percentage point, this would reduce 2030 coal demand by an amount almost equal to the volume currently consumed by the whole of Europe. Oil import volumes would decline by 5% and LNG imports by more than 20%, with major implications for global balances."

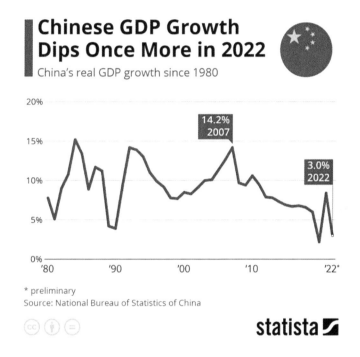

Chart 6: Chinese GDP Growth Dips, National Bureau of Statistics of China

Chinese leadership has guided the empire from a state of poverty at the end of World War II to (arguably) a developed first world nation. For thirty years China has been a major driver in the world economy and given Chinese oil production has not been able to quench the associated insatiable demand, the rest of the world benefited from that demand. Clearly that pace has slowed and it is widely expected that Chinese GDP will grow around 3.5% until 2030, this is reflected in the expected demand for fossil fuels (see Chart 5.)

I have included figures 13, 14, and executive summary 19 for you to get a handle on the scope of the decline in demand created by the evolution of the Chinese economy. For the most part Canada did not exploit its full energy supply potential which is the basis that the Federal Government used to sell TMX and CGL pipelines to the Canadian public. Now that the Canadian Government has wasted around 40 billion CAD by building into a falling demand curve,

I suggest we learn from our mistakes by looking around and see what is actually happening and proactively helping others by helping ourselves. Again create the crown corporation tasked with the proliferation of green hydrogen domestically at first and secondly for export.

India

India is further behind China in the overall development of the country and as a result it is widely expected their demand for fossil fuels will continue to increase in the short term but that is only a projection. Their National Green Hydrogen Mission has lofty export goals which require a significant private sector pickup. With the Indian population being very similar to Chinas', the potential is Huge, but given that fossil fuels are still the cheapest way of producing baseline energy, the projections will likely hold true.

5.9.1 Key energy and emissions trends

Figure 5.23 ▷ Key trends in India, 2010-2050

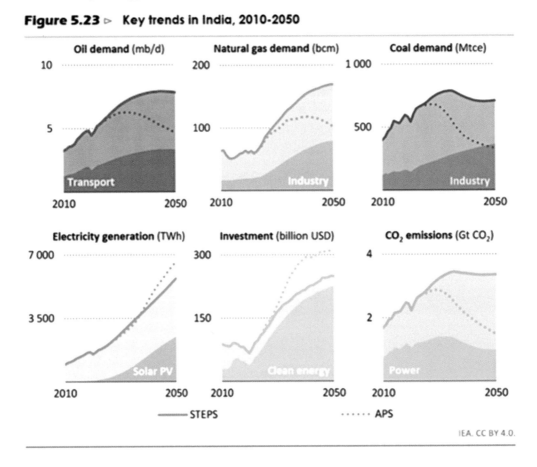

Chart 7: Key trends in India, 2010 - 2050, International Energy Agency

The European Union

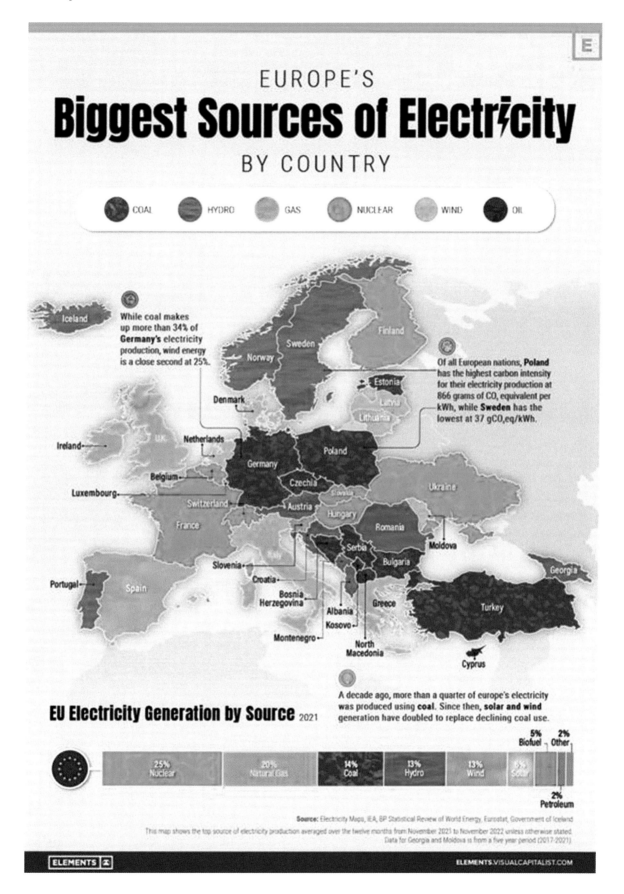

5.4   European Union

5.4.1   *Key energy and emissions trends*

Figure 5.7 ▷   **Key trends in the European Union, 2010-2050**

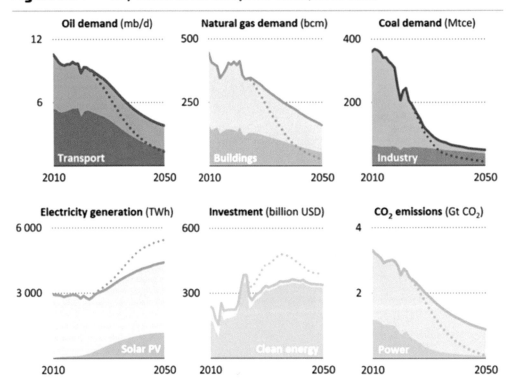

Chart 8: Key trends in the European Union, 2010 -2050 International Energy Agency

With the break-out of war in the Ukraine, and the resulting effects on the supply of Russian Energy, energy security is a high priority within the EU at this time. As noted earlier, EU leaders made it a priority to visit Canada hoping to secure an alternate safe, reliable supply of energy without success. As I write, French energy giant Total recently released a tender for 500,000 tons of green hydrogen per annum, likely filled by a European or an American company. The EU, like almost every other developed nation (other than Canada), has dedicated significant time and resources planning and has dedicated significant time and resources, planning and building green infrastructure to support their energy needs.

5.10   Japan and Korea

5.10.1   Key energy and emissions trends

Figure 5.27 ▷ **Key trends in Japan and Korea, 2010-2050**

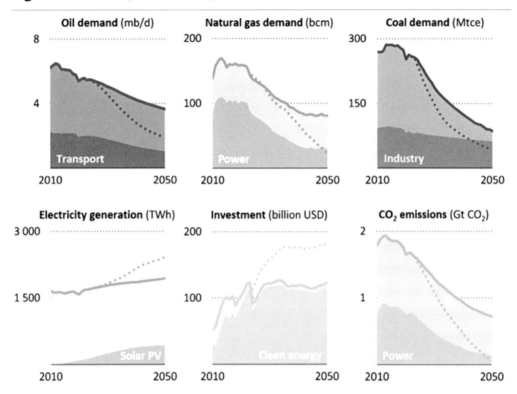

Chart 9: Key trends in Japan and Korea, 2010 – 2050, International Energy Agency

Table 5.11 ▷ **Key policy initiatives in Japan and Korea**

Policy	Description
Japan: Basic Hydrogen Strategy (updated in 2023)	• Aims to accelerate public and private investment in the hydrogen supply chain with JPY 15 trillion (USD 114 billion) over the next 15 years. • Plans to install around 15 GW of electrolysers by Japanese companies both domestically and abroad by 2030.
Japan: Green Transformation (GX) basic policy	• Aims to achieve decarbonisation, energy security and economic growth with public and private investment of JPY 150 trillion (USD 1 trillion) over the next ten years. • Intends to fund the promotion of renewable energy, i.e. R&D offshore wind cost reduction, and transition, i.e. building mass hydrogen supply chain, and extend the lifetime of existing nuclear reactors.
Korea: 10th Basic Plan for Long-term Electricity Supply and Demand	• Seeks to increase the share of renewables and nuclear – a shift from previous phase-out plans – in the power mix to 31% and 35% respectively and reduce the share of coal to 15% by 2036. • Plans to expand the power generation capacity from 148 GW level in 2023 to 239 GW by 2036.
Korea: 1st National Basic Plan for Carbon Neutrality and Green Growth	• Includes 2023 NDC updates of the 2021 NDC which maintains the same GHG reduction target at 40% from 2018 levels but with adjusted sectoral targets. • Intends to strengthen the power sector reduction target to 45.9% by 2030 from 2018 levels, with increased roles for nuclear and renewables, and to reduce the target for the industry sector to a 11.4% cut by 2030 from 14.5% in the previous NDC.

Note: JPY = Japanese yen; NDC = Nationally Determined Contribution.

Table 3: Key policy initiatives in Japan and Korea, International Energy Agency

5.10.3 What role can hydrogen play in the energy mix and how can the governments deploy it?

In the APS, Japan and Korea import significant quantities of hydrogen and hydrogen-based fuels for use in the power sector and for direct use in industry. By 2050, Korea and Japan account for almost 40% of global hydrogen imports (Figure 5.29).

Figure 5.29 ▷ **Imported hydrogen and hydrogen-based fuels in the APS, 2030 and 2050**

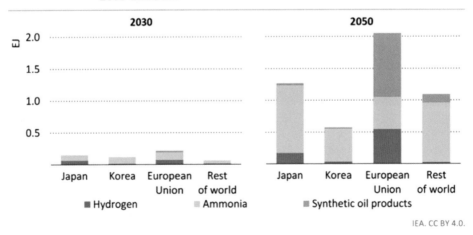

Japan and Korea become the second-largest importers of hydrogen and hydrogen-based fuels after the European Union

Table 4: Hydrogen Imports and Hydrogen based fuels, International Energy Agency

WAR

(War) it ain't <u>nothing</u> but a heart-breaker
(War) <u>friend</u> only to the undertaker
Oh, war it's an <u>enemy</u> to all mankind
The <u>point</u> of war <u>blows</u> my mind
War has <u>caused</u> unrest
Within the <u>younger</u> generation
Induction then destruction
Who <u>wants</u> to die, ah, war-huh, good god why'all
What is it good for
Absolutely nothing

-Edwin Starr, *War*

I encourage you to read or listen to Edwin's awesomely accurate depiction of war and I submit to you that a large component of humanity's evolution involves realizing that war does nothing but impede civilizations' progress by:

- Unnecessarily sapping resources.
- Diverting our focus.
- Unnecessarily maintaining division for the purpose of control.

All resulting in slower or negligible growth with respect to our evolution as intelligent beings.

I suggest that we collectively focus on team building activities such as:

- solving climate change to ensure that we all have a safe, stable footing from which to flourish.
- providing clean energy to everyone globally.
- making poverty a thing of the past.
- finding ways to expand our civilization, not tear it apart for the minority's financial gain.

Make no mistake! War itself is a crime and we should abolish the Geneva Convention.

Giving a set of rules to this mortal game gives a false impression of morality to politicians and people getting rich from it (is the number one goal REGARDLESS of whatever propaganda they are toting.) They campaign whatever excuse they want to the rest of the world (oppression, religious persecution, land ownership, being spied on) because there is a set of accepted rules. If you accept that killing another human being is just an all-round bad idea then doing so in any situation is unacceptable.

It should come as no surprise that the small people who become world leaders might resort to engaging in violent behavior with their neighbors to resolve an issue and could claim that they are playing by societal rules. Conflict is detrimental from all perspectives yet people that are not desperate still elect to try and solve a problem (perceived or not) with violence. Evidently, more time seems to be needed to remove ineffectual leaders who still resort to using our most basic of instincts.

Russia's war on Ukraine

No matter the history, Russia unnecessarily initiated the violence and is therefore at fault for the current conflict and its consequences.

It is now apparent that fossil fuel sanctions are not working and likely never will because The cost of producing oil in Russia is less than in the U.S. and much less than in the Canadian oil sands. A lack of demand for their product will stop Russian exports, GUARANTEED.

Hastening the demise of fossil fuels **will** have the following effects on this atrocious conflict, it will:

1. bring Russia to the negotiating table.
2. mitigate climate change.
3. drive research and development by creating competition. (I assure you the race will heat up)
4. create energy security for those who switch and a more restrictive atmosphere for anyone contemplating violence against one's neighbour.

Make no mistake, we are at war with ourselves and indirectly with Russia. To triumph over Russia without direct involvement we need to significantly decrease our oil demand while helping others to do the same.

WHY CANADA?

———◄○►———

The short answer – because we used to be -and can be again- PROUD of our contributions to society.

I have watched the current Canadian leadership outright lie to Canadians and embarrass us internationally with their antics. Canadian politicians recognize that Canada's democracy is failing and in 2015 Justin Trudeau promised that if they were elected, they would institute electoral reform, meaningfully start to address climate change and stop the bombing of Syria. They did have other policy initiatives, but I felt these 3 topics were the primary issues of the day. Does anyone aim to achieve only 33% of their goals? That is all the Trudeau Government could manage. After studying the subject of electoral reform, they reported to Canadians that they were not going to do that. Since taking power in 2015, along with steady increase of carbon emissions, the production of fossil fuels has continued to increase. However, they did manage to stop the use of the Canadian military to bomb Syria. One for 3 isn't bad!!! Would you settle for a 33% success rate? Would any business? I argue that all the legacy Canadian political parties would have you settle for this because they either lack the imagination, political will, or foresight.

In 2022, Chancellor Shulz came to Canada looking to secure energy (I can't remember the last time a German Chancellor came to visit Canada) and sadly Trudeau did his best to embarrass us by sending him packing with meaningless promises.

In 2023, EU President Ursula Von Der Leyen also came to visit looking to discuss our common problems - with an emphasis on the Russia / Ukraine war. Likely aware of the response Shulz got that securing more energy was not going happen, she seemingly focused more on military and monetary aid for Ukraine, which Trudeau actually delivered…. You probably thought I was going to call him out on another failure of his, no, I give credit where it is due.

During our brief history, our Canadian forebearers accomplished tasks that others were not able to earning a reputation as peacekeepers, and were innovators who kept up with the best the world had to offer.

During WWI (and again in WWII) our ancestors were called upon to achieve the unachievable - the battles of Passchendaele and Vimy Ridge being great examples. In the 50's Lester B. Pearson created a peace plan for the cessation of hostilities around the Suez Canal internationally cementing our reputation as international peacekeepers.

Throughout our country's short existence Canadians have contributed to humanities evolution by:

- discovering insulin
- inventing the portable external pacemaker

- being the 1st country to use satellites to communicate,
- and creating the Canadarm for the shuttle program
  to name a few.

The challenges are many and their size is daunting, but I believe that we can rise to the challenge and help humanity into what should be the next phase of our evolution by working together with one another and our environment.

Canada has all the wealth necessary to build the infrastructure and the educational base to catch up with our competitors and then take the lead. Due to the size of the country, population, and high level of Education, it is within our capacity to produce significant amounts of green hydrogen for export. We can profit from good jobs at home while creating jobs abroad and increasing our revenues from exports. As with all other technologies, the more we use them the cheaper they will be.

To coincide with domestic operations we can work with others to build foreign hydrogen power plants and supply them. For example, the U.S. under President Biden, has significantly invested in a hydrogen economy, making the resurrection of Keystone XL pipeline highly probable if it were designed to carry green hydrogen.

ENERGY MARKET FORECAST

In November 2023 the Canadian Energy Regulator (CER) released a report on Canada's Energy Future.

Nearly all hydrogen consumed today is grey hydrogen (approximately 90 million tons[1] per annum [Mtpa]).

I have seen green hydrogen demand projections increase from 125 and 585 Mtpa by 2050.

at best 650% over 25 years equals a <u>growth</u> rate of 26% per annum.

at worst 38% over 25 years equals a <u>growth</u> rate of 1.5% per annum.

These numbers (being projections) can be altered by any number of positive and negative stimuli. We have recently seen significant push back against switching to clean energy as noted by O.P.E.C.'s 2024 data driven projection out to 2045 showing an increase of 16% over 21 years which is 1.3% per annum. I have also seen many world demand projections for fossil fuel use out to 2050 decline by 20% and 60%.

The day that I submitted this manuscript I felt blessed to be able to share this projection published in the journal Nature. *"The economic commitment of climate change"* by <u>Maximilian Kotz</u>, • <u>Anders Levermann</u> & • <u>Leonie Wenz</u> is a study using various conservative models they estimate the losses due to climate change in 2049 (17).They estimate it will cost the global economy 38 trillion USD per annum compared to a global economy that does not suffer from climate change.

Assuming a population of roughly (based on 1% growth rate) 10 billion people on the planet in 2049 that works out to 3800.00 USD per capita unnecessary loss due to climate change.

CONCLUSION

I bow to no one whom i do not consider worthy, but if that is what it takes to get you to vote green, I beg you in the name of my child, your children, and the children to come vote green and potentially change the course of history. Ask me to build a green hydrogen economy and with your help (and that of the Canadian Federal Government), I'll make it happen.

Now more than ever we need leadership! We need a focus and a goal. If I were elected Member of Parliament (MP), at the first opportunity I would propose a bill that would cut MP's salary by 20% to reflect the awful decisions they have made during the past 8 years followed by the creation of a Crown Corporation tasked with the creation of a green hydrogen economy. Let's focus on building the green hydrogen economy creating significant overcapacity as orders come in.

If I were to meet Justin Trudeau I would address him as Mr. Trudeau, or Justin if he preferred, but I would not be able to use the prefix "Prime Minister" because he has not earned it. Despite the egregious divisions that exist in Western society currently I believe now more than ever we need leadership. President Biden has provided some leadership, however, for all the good he has done he has possibly jeopardized it all by turning a blind eye to the war in Gaza.

Consider the results of the 2 different paths:

Path 1

Continuation of fossil fuel proliferation with green washing to help steer us down the path of destruction until it is too late to change course guaranteeing job losses, further environmental degradation, and no chance of climate change mitigation.

Path 2

Embrace green energy! at best: creating the good long term jobs, mitigate effects of climate change, help others achieve energy security, be leaders in the new economy, at worst: we will meet our Paris agreement targets, we will have expensive energy, slow and /or stop environmental degradation, achieve energy independence (stop importing oil) and be in a position to help others do the same, some long term jobs.

Green energy is the next step in our evolution!

How would the rest of the world view Canadians if we were able to supply the rest of the world with clean energy.

Why are we allowing climate change to worsen?

The technology exists today, what we are lacking is the individual resolve to act. Despite showing an achievable path that, at best results in:

-the gradual reversal of climate change

-a considerable increase in jobs

-significant goodwill

-and monetary wealth

At worst results in:

-progressive jobs

-goodwill

-and a large amount of green hydrogen

monetary wealth; at worst by providing Canadians with progressive jobs, goodwill (by exceeding our targets) and a large amount of green hydrogen. Switching to renewable energy is a **guaranteed win** and the longer we depend on fossil fuel energy the larger the **losses will be.** Now it is only a matter of how big that loss will be**.**

Many people who read these arguments will only see that I plan to make the fossil fuel industry pay for the transition by raising their taxes and that will be enough to trigger the realization that most of the wealth stored in the Canadian capital markets will take a hit sooner than when your kid is scheduled to attend University and you don't want to give up those nice dividends.

Despite all the above arguments and logic, it is likely that you are still clinging to that one argument that nullifies your acceptance (yes I am going to vote green!) and that is why I have assigned a 95% probability of continuing with the status quo. There is an unlimited number of excuses as to why a person might not vote for the Green Party of Canada, the U.S. Green Party or Cornel West, and they are all just that, excuses. Our very home is being "burnt" down! All other considerations are irrelevant! Most Christians are familiar with the prayer closing "world without end;" yes, the planet (maybe our species) will continue but in what manner? How much suffering will occur before we break the hold dirty energy has on us and our society?

Assuming that messages like this go unheeded and inaction wins the day, it is fortunate that the younger generations will be better equipped to think about new ways of doing things; it seems that they see our hypocrisy. I don't know a parent that has not noticed that the listening skills of our children are horrendous.

Why should they listen?

Many of us say that we have their best interests at heart but our actions say otherwise.

The suffering has not yet become intolerable to everyone and so apathy, tax cuts, nepotism, individualism, and capitalism will continue to rule the day.

Even though I suggested a path that guarantees more jobs and wealth, as well as a higher probability of peace, I estimate that there is only a 5% chance that we will be able to bring these arguments to the broader public before the planet's thermal moderators disappear.

What will it be? Who are you really?

Guaranteed win? Guaranteed Loss?

We shall see....

Be Seeing You

richard

REFERENCES

1. https://www.cbc.ca/news/canada/calgary/alberta-renewables-pause-ending-soon-1.7105233
2. https://www.cbc.ca/news/science/fossil-fuel-subsidies-expaliner-1.6371411
3. https://www.space.com/17816-earth-temperature.html
4. https://climate.nasa.gov/news/2740/climate-change-may-lead-to-bigger-atmospheric-rivers/
5. https://www.cbc.ca/player/play/2071443011551
6. https://www.cbc.ca/news/politics/trudeau-electoral-reform-1.7101929
7. https://globalnews.ca/video/6025449/federal-election-2019-singh-says-he-remains-opposed-to-trans-mountain-pipeline-expansion/#:~:text=During%20a%20%E2%80%9CGet%20out%20the%20Vote%E2%80%9D%20event%20in,be%20continuing%20to%20be%20opposed%20to%20it%20tomorr
8. https://www.cbc.ca/news/canada/edmonton/alberta-whistleblower-fort-chipewyan-john-o-connor-1.5943389
9. https://www.nationalgeographic.com/environment/article/alberta-canadas-tar-sands-is-growing-but-indigenous-people-fight-back
10. 10. https://www.aptnnews.ca/national-news/first-nation-bc-trans-mountain-pipeline-through-sacred-site/
11. https://www.pbo-dpb.ca/en/publications/RP-2223-011-S--trans-mountain-pipeline-update--reseau-pipelines-trans-mountain-mise-jour
12. https://www.webmd.com/balance/what-is-a-type-a-personality
13. https://www.newsnationnow.com/on-balance-with-leland-vittert/vittert-the-dc-revolving-door-is-now-shameless/
14. https://www.health.harvard.edu/blog/the-truth-about-altruism-201601058929
15. https://www.cbc.ca/news/politics/budget-officer-trans-mountain-expansion-1.6497263
16. https://www.pbo-dpb.ca/en/publications/RP-2223-011-S--trans-mountain-pipeline-update--
17. https://ca.finance.yahoo.com/news/suncor-tweaks-worker-pay-ceo-to-keep-focus-on-elimination-of-work-in-2024-200810972.html
18. https://www.nature.com/articles/s41467-022-35419-7

ABOUT THE AUTHOR

I grew up in small town Manitoba playing high-level hockey, and participating in most sports available in school. I graduated from the University of Manitoba with a bachelor of Arts, focusing heavily on History and Macro-economics.

I then spent a lengthy 13 years in the financial industry finishing most of the certificates offered by the Canadian Securities Institute at the time. During this time I climbed the corporate ladder as high as an assistant Branch Manager. I have exercised my talent in such high profiles as: RBC, TD, and two private brokerage firms while providing a Commodities focused radio commentary for five years airing across western Canada.

In 2006 I was the Conservative candidate for Member of Parliament for Winnipeg Centre.

In 2011 I was unable to justify who I was, with what I was doing and thus left the financial industry. A good friend of mine I had worked with in the mining industry employed me as a geophysics technician until I left in 2015 to be near my child, at which time I took a job doing concrete forming in the Vancouver lower mainland. In 2019 my back had had enough so I started my current occupation of commercial electrician.

Upon my arrival in the lower mainland I was prompted to action by the proposal to twin the TMX; I helped organize the 2016 march that drove Kinder Morgan out of Canada. I have been actively opposing our government's energy policies ever since recognizing that business as usual no longer exists.

Printed in the United States
by Baker & Taylor Publisher Services